I0410388

RECREATION & TOURISM INITIATIVE

Place-Based Planning: Innovations and Applications From Four Western Forests

General Technical Report
PNW-GTR-741
April 2008

 United States
Department of
Agriculture

 Forest
Service

PNW Pacific Northwest
Research Station

Editors

Jennifer O. Farnum was a research social scientist, Pacific Wildland Fire Sciences Laboratory, 400 N 34th St., Suite 201, Seattle, WA 98107. **Linda E. Kruger** is a research social scientist, Forestry Sciences Laboratory, 2770 Sherwood Lane Suite, 2A, Juneau, AK 99801.

Place-Based Planning: Innovations and Applications From Four Western Forests

Jennifer O. Farnum and Linda E. Kruger

Editors

U.S. Department of Agriculture, Forest Service

Pacific Northwest Research Station

Portland, OR

General Technical Report PNW-GTR-741

April 2008

Abstract

Farnum, Jennifer O.; Kruger, Linda E., eds. 2008. Place-based planning: innovations and applications from four western forests. Gen. Tech. Rep. PNW-GTR-741. Portland, OR: U.S. Department of Agriculture, Forest Service, Pacific Northwest Research Station. 44 p.

Place-based planning is an emergent method of public lands planning that aims to redefine the scale at which planning occurs, using place meanings and place values to guide planning processes. Despite the approach's growing popularity, there exist few published accounts of place-based approaches. To provide practitioners and researchers with such examples, the current compilation outlines the historical background, planning rationale, and public involvement processes from four National Forest System areas: The Beaverhead-Deerlodge National Forest in Montana; the Willamette National Forest in Oregon; the Chugach National Forest in Alaska; and the Grand Mesa, Uncompahgre, and Gunnison National Forests in Colorado. These examples include assessments of the successes and challenges encountered in each approach.

Keywords: Collaboration, forest planning, place attachment, place-based planning, public values, sense of place.

Contents

Chapter 1: An Introduction to Place-Based Planning

Linda E. Kruger

Exploring New Approaches to Forest Planning

"Place-based planning" refers to land and natural resource planning efforts that bring together diverse human values, uses, experiences, and activities tied to specific geographic locations. Although planning efforts have always focused on specific places through land use zoning frameworks, place-based planning is different from other types of approaches. For example, whereas land use zoning segregates dominant uses from one another on the landscape, place-based planning takes a more holistic approach, focusing on identifying current uses, values, and meanings. In addition, place-based approaches tend to take a longitudinal perspective, exploring desired future conditions for the landscape. This approach enables participants to identify a variety of uses that might occur concurrently rather than designating one primary use for the upcoming 10 to 20 years.

Land managers use a variety of processes, activities, and forums to identify and spatially depict how people value and use landscapes. Forest plan revision, a process required by the 1976 National Forest Management Act (NFMA), has enabled place-based techniques to emerge on forests throughout the National Forest System. Although there are many innovative place-based approaches, there is little in the way of summary and synthesis of these approaches. The purpose of this report is to provide examples of place-based planning with an emphasis on practical applications, tools, and techniques. First we explore some foundational concepts underlying this approach.

> **Place values are important components of the way people appreciate, enjoy, and experience the environment.**

Foundational Concepts

Place-oriented approaches to natural resource and community issues are receiving increasing attention from academics, policymakers, citizens, and resource managers (see Farnum et al. 2005). The concepts of sense of place, attachment to place, and place-based planning are appearing more frequently in academic literature, agency publications, and the popular press. This attention is indicative of the fact that place values are important components of the way people appreciate, enjoy, and experience the environment (Ehrendfeld 1993, Norton and Hannon 1997).

Place is a multidimensional term used by social scientists in four ways; these four conceptions are used independently and in combination with each other to express and understand the multiple meanings and uses of a place (Agnew and Duncan 1989). **As location**, place refers to the way social and economic activities spatially occur on the land. Place as **locale** recognizes place as the setting or backdrop for everyday activities. **Sense of place** involves individual or group identification with a place that comes from personally interacting with it and experiencing it with one's senses. This type of identification with a place can result in appreciation and attachment beyond the observable features of the landscape (i.e., **place attachment**).

We suggest that **existence attachment** can be used to describe a concept related to place attachment, a term that refers to an appreciation of and attachment to a place that one has not experienced first hand.[1] Thus, existence attachment is a concept closely akin to **existence value**, a concept in environmental economics that has long been used as a method for valuing lands (Krutilla 1967). Existence value is predicated on the idea that the knowledge of natural resources' existence is in its own right an important benefit of maintaining such resources (e.g., Fredman 1995). Thus, people with strong sentiments toward places they have never visited (e.g., Yellowstone National Park or the Galapagos Islands) can be said to have existence attachment (often owing to an area's symbolic or cultural value), whereas the land itself can be said to hold existence value.

Place-Based Planning Processes

Slowly, sometimes in fits and starts, planning processes have begun to recognize the importance of place attachment—the emotional ties and feelings of connectedness that people have for places—and the intangible (e.g., cultural, symbolic, and spiritual) meanings and values people ascribe to places (Galliano and Loeffler 1999). Place-related concepts are becoming better understood, and managers are finding value in the contribution these concepts make to planning and management applications (Norton and Hannon 1998).

An essential idea behind place-based planning is that caring about **places** is important and different from caring about **resources** (Mitchell et al. 1993). There is a difference between valuing a resource (or even what some might call a type of place such as wilderness) and valuing a place that might contain that resource or belong to that particular type of place. Place-based planning brings to bear the

---

[1] Thanks to Dale Blahna for help in differentiating existence attachment from sense of place.

meanings, values, and attachments associated with a specific location in addition to any meaning it might have as a type of place or container of a resource.

Understanding the significant meanings that places have for individuals and groups may enable planners, managers, and decisionmakers to develop management guidelines that preserve the characteristics that make those places important (Galiano and Loeffler 1999). Thus, place-based planning provides an opportunity to:

- Empower community members and build camaraderie.
- Establish positive relationships and trust.
- Enable participants (both from the agency and the public) to regain credibility that may have been diminished or lost in previous planning activities.
- Engage in mutual learning.
- Explain policies and rationale.
- Surface and mitigate conflict.
- Plan holistically.
- Incorporate a broad range of place meanings into planning and management.
- Focus on stakeholder similarities rather than differences.
- Encourage positive outcomes by addressing underlying sources of conflict.

Considerations in Using Place-Based Planning Processes

Place-based planning processes allow managers to interact with people who live, work, and play in a place and who care about it. This is important because planning in itself is a place-making or meaning-creating process (Galliano and Loeffler 1999; Williams and Patterson 1996, 1999). Place-based planning engages the public and enables an understanding of what Clarke (1971, quoted in Galiano and Loeffler 1999) calls "the interactive unity of people and place."

Although in theory meaning can be mapped like other spatial properties, there are at least two problems with identifying and mapping intangible meanings. First, by definition, intangible meanings leave few (if any) physical indicators, behavioral evidence, or cultural markers in the landscape to indicate they exist. Second, places typically do not have a single set of meanings held by everyone (Greider and Garkovich 1994). For managers to identify the full range of meanings requires an expanded set of inventory techniques that are capable of identifying intangible meanings and that are sensitive to the social or group differences in such meanings (Kruger and Williams 2007).

Knowledge of the politics of place can help managers understand natural resource conflict and better evaluate the potential effectiveness of decision-making processes.

In addition to mapping components or activities, place-based approaches also frequently involve a visioning exercise. Visioning is intended to "create…more equitable, democratic ways of defining, expressing, and valuing places" (Cheng et al. 2003: 101). It is seen as a way to build relationships and share power, and acknowledges that a "one-size-fits-all" planning template is inappropriate because it does not recognize the uniqueness of each landscape and situation.

Knowledge of the politics of place can help managers understand natural resource conflict and better evaluate the potential effectiveness of decisionmaking processes. Understanding contested meanings of place is important for managers because sense of place, existence attachment, and place meanings are expressed through attitudes and expectations about appropriate and inappropriate management or use (Cheng et al. 2003).

Case Description Format

A workshop on place-based planning was held on November 5–7, 2003, in Portland, Oregon, to provide a venue for Forest Service planners and others to share their experiences in implementing place-oriented planning techniques. The goal of the workshop was to increase awareness about how place-based approaches have been applied and the unique benefits and challenges associated with each one.

Workshop attendees were identified through word-of-mouth and prior work with the Pacific Northwest Research Station. Participants came from Alaska, California, Colorado, Idaho, Montana, Utah, and Washington. The current collection consists of four short vignettes, all of which were presented at the workshop.

This collection contributes to our understanding of how place-based approaches are being applied across a variety of divergent biophysical settings and sociocultural environments. We worked closely with managers and others involved in the projects to present their approaches as honestly and transparently as possible. Our hope is that these vignettes will provide managers and research scientists with additional insight into the role place plays in how people relate to the land. Providing tangible, application-oriented examples of these approaches allows us to continue to build a community of managers and researchers who can help further best practices.

Literature Cited

Agnew, J.A.; Duncan, J.S. 1989. Introduction. In: Agnew, J.A.; Duncan, J.S., eds. The power of place. Boston: Unwin Hyman: 1–8.

Cheng, A.S.; Kruger, L.E.; Daniels, S.E. 2003. "Place" as an integrating concept in natural resource politics: propositions for a social science research agenda. Society and Natural Resources. 16(2): 87–104.

Clarke, W.C. 1971. Place and people: an ecology of a New Guinean community. Berkeley, CA: University of California Press. 127 p.

Ehrenfeld, D. 1993. Beginning again: people and nature in the new millennium. New York: Oxford University Press. 240 p.

Farnum, J.O.; Hall, T.E.; Kruger, L.E. 2005. Sense of place in natural resources recreation and tourism: an evaluation and assessment of research findings. Gen. Tech. Rep. PNW-GTR-660. Portland, OR: U.S. Department of Agriculture, Forest Service, Pacific Northwest Research Station. 59 p.

Fredman, P. 1995. The existence of existence value—a study of the economic benefits of an endangered species. Journal of Forest Economics. 1(3): 307–327.

Galliano, S.J.; Loeffler, G.M. 1999. Place attachments: how people define eco-systems. Gen. Tech. Rep. PNW-GTR-462. Portland, OR: U.S. Department of Agriculture, Forest Service, Pacific Northwest Research Station. 31 p.

Greider, T.; Garkovich, L. 1994. Landscapes: the social construction of nature and the environment. Rural Sociology. 59(1): 1–24.

Kruger, L.E.; Williams, D.R. 2007. Place and place-based planning. In: Kruger, L.E.; Mazza, R.; Lawrence, K., eds. Proceedings: national workshop on recreation research and management. Gen. Tech. Rep. PNW-GTR-698. Portland, OR: U.S. Department of Agriculture, Forest Service, Pacific Northwest Research Station: 83–88.

Krutilla, J.V. 1967. Conservation reconsidered. The American Economic Review. 57: 777–786.

Mitchell, M.Y.; Force, J.E.; Carroll, M.S.; McLaughlin, W.J. 1993. Forest places of the heart. Journal of Forestry. 91(4): 32–37.

Norton, B.G.; Hannon, B. 1997. Environmental values: a place-based theory. Environmental Ethics. 19(4): 227–245.

Norton, B.G.; Hannon, B. 1998. Democracy and sense of place values in environmental policy. In: Light, A.; Smith, J.M., eds. Philosophy and geography III: philosophies of place. Lanhan, MD: Rowman and Littlefield Publishers Inc: 119–145.

Williams, D.R.; Patterson, M.E. 1996. Environmental meaning and ecosystem management: perspectives from environmental psychology and human geography. Society and Natural Resources. 9(5): 507–521.

Williams, D.R.; Patterson, M.E. 1999. Environmental psychology: mapping landscape meanings for ecosystem management. In: Cordell, H.K.; Bergstrom, J.C., eds. Integrating social sciences and ecosystem management: human dimensions in assessment, policy and management. Champaign, IL: Sagamore Press: 141–160.

Chapter 2: The Beaverhead-Deerlodge National Forest

Jennifer O. Farnum, Anita DeZort, and Janet Bean-Dochnahl

Overview of the Area

The Beaverhead-Deerlodge National Forest (BDNF) is in the southwestern corner of Montana, surrounded by the communities of Dillon, Ennis, Butte, Boulder, and Deerlodge. The landscape consists of mountain ranges separated by valleys, towns, and agricultural areas. A variety of forest densities can be found on the BDNF (i.e., from heavily to sparsely forested) as well as large areas of grasslands.

The 3.32-million-acre forest is noncontiguous, interspersed with U.S. Department of the Interior, Bureau of Land Management, and privately owned parcels. The BDNF is home to two wilderness areas (Anaconda-Pintler and Lee Metcalf) and two proposed wilderness areas (West Pioneers and Sapphires). A variety of recreational activities are popular on the BDNF including snowmobiling, skiing, hiking, and scenic driving.

The history of the BDNF area is one of its most prominent characteristics. Before settlement by nonindigenous people, the land served as a main crossroads for Native American tribes. Shortly after the arrival of nonindigenous people in the mid-1800s, the railroad was introduced to the area, which had a lasting effect on the area's culture and settlement patterns. At about the same time, mining assumed an important role in the region's economic base. Today, mining continues to be a major player in culture and economy; ranching and grazing, too, have become mainstays in the region.

Project Rationale

When this project was first initiated in the early 1990s, the BDNF region was experiencing growth on two fronts: (1) migration of newcomers to the small communities surrounding the forest, newcomers moving to the area to experience the "Rocky Mountain West;" and (2) rising levels of tourism in Montana. The BDNF's location between two major interstates, Interstate 90 and Interstate 15, contributed to the influx of both new residents and tourists.

The BDNF planners and managers recognized that changes in seasonal and year-round populations would inevitably lead to changes in communities' cultures

Planners and managers recognized that changes in seasonal and year-round populations would inevitably lead to changes in communities' cultures and, by extension, land management priorities.

and, by extension, land management priorities. Producing a forest plan that incorporated the dynamic nature of community needs and preferences required a departure from traditional, static, expert-driven planning processes.

The BDNF also felt pressure to produce a first-rate forest plan because of contention that had arisen during previous planning processes. In the two previous forest planning endeavors, management areas had been very small and determined by criteria driven by the biophysical sciences for the purposes of timber production. Management areas were so small that they were challenging for the public to visualize. As a result, difficulty was encountered in developing shared understandings of the area, inevitably hindering communication between the U.S. Department of Agriculture, Forest Service and the public. Disputes between the public and the agency ensued and relationships became strained. Thus, the goal of this approach was to simultaneously recognize preexisting concerns while being attuned to new values, beliefs, and social structures that were arising as a result of changing populations. To do so, planners focused on identifying the public's priorities for the BDNF and rescaling management area boundaries to make them more meaningful.

Methods, Techniques, and Participants

When the BDNF first began to consider its upcoming forest plan revision, the idea of place-based planning or socially driven management approaches was not as developed as it is today. Because there was little precedent for such approaches, BDNF planners adopted an adaptive management style that allowed for flexibility within their general planning framework.

The initial task that planners undertook was to segment the forest into large parcels of land, or forest **landscapes**. The goals of segmentation were to make the revision process more manageable and, at the same time, better represent the scale of people's attachments to public lands. A total of 12 forest landscapes were identified by looking at the forest's distinctive geographical features and clustering areas accordingly (see fig. 1).

Once landscape boundaries were drawn, the next step in the planning process was to generate landscape descriptions that captured biophysical and social qualities. Thus, forest inventories—or **landscape assessments**—were initiated to gather information about the forest's physical, social, and cultural resources.

To lead the landscape assessment process, teams of stakeholders were recruited from a variety of organizations. Teams comprised members of the public; representatives from the BLM; employees of Montana Fish, Wildlife, and Parks; resource specialists; and representatives from forest districts. Teams first collected data to

Figure 1   The 12 landscapes identified for the Beaverhead Deerlodge
National Forest.

determine landscapes' resource potential, looking at such factors as range of vegetation, watershed quality, and historical human uses. By looking at existing information and sharing expertise, teams evaluated the landscapes' current conditions
and tried to determine how much those conditions differed from historical conditions. Teams sought to gauge how the forest had evolved and how the biological,
social, and cultural constitution of the area would likely change (i.e., the forest's
future conditions).

To better understand the social and cultural constitution of landscapes, the
public was consulted regularly. The way in which this occurred varied depending
on the availability of resources and the interest level of BDNF staff. In some cases,
informal discussions were initiated based on ranger district personnel's knowledge
of communities. Arguably, this technique may not have captured an accurate cross-
section of public sentiment. However, other techniques were more inclusive and
methodical. Public meetings—at least initially—seemed to attract a diversity of
people and options. Representatives from federal and state agencies, county government, the Montana Wilderness Association, the Montana Logging Association,
grazing associations, chambers of commerce—all attended these well-advertised
meetings.

For the public meetings, Forest Service staff underwent specialized training in facilitation; thus, they were able to lead meaningful discussions that provided the BDNF with a clearer idea of public priorities and attachments to forest places. Participants were encouraged to think about what determines a "place," what distinct places exist on the BDNF, what places mean to them, and, based on these meanings, the appropriate uses for places both currently and in the future.

Partway into the planning process, a Montana Consensus Council survey revealed that many people had grown weary of public meetings and wanted different forums to provide input. To accommodate this preference, the BDNF arranged for the forest planner to provide presentations and receive feedback about the planning products (i.e., planning documents) and processes at various venues. This format of sharing information was appreciated, and hundreds of presentations were made to interested parties. Ultimately, citizens were highly involved in 3 of the 12 landscapes assessments; changes in funding and the political climate prevented full public involvement in the remaining nine landscapes.

As a result of the sentiments expressed at meetings and presentations, the landscape assessments reflected participants' place meanings and place attachments. Although multiple forest uses were discussed in the assessments, the assessments were organized around the quality that was most valued by the largest number of people—the forest's recreational capacity.

During the course of landscape assessments, it became clear that the landscapes themselves—while smaller in scale than the entire forest—were still too large to develop targeted recommendations that accurately captured the public's place meanings and attachments. Meetings and presentation feedback continually reinforced the idea that citizens thought of the forest at a finer scale than larger "landscapes" permitted. Planners also recognized that they needed to generate products that met National Environmental Policy Act (NEPA) and forest plan requirements. Thus, smaller, more discrete management areas were carved out of the larger landscapes, which in turn were intended to lay the groundwork for developing forest planning documents.

The process of deriving management areas from landscapes rested on a detailed evaluation of public input and zoning area considerations. To avoid some of the problems with management area zoning that had been encountered in previous forest plan revisions, several criteria were employed including (1) management area boundaries must be identifiable on the ground, (2) the recreation setting must be similar throughout the area, and (3) management priorities should be fairly uniform across the identified area. When evaluating these criteria, planners also considered

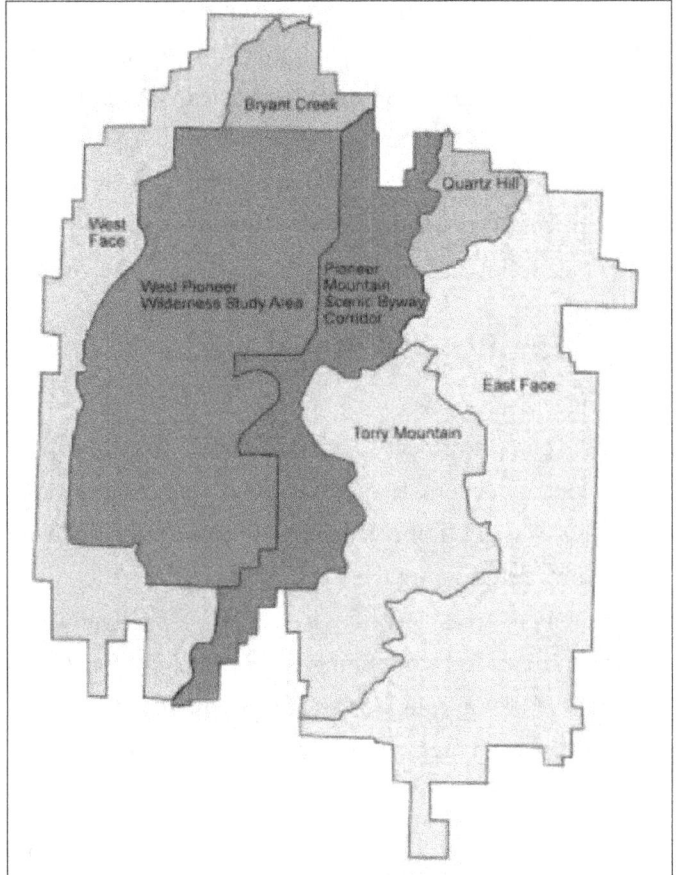

Figure 2   Management areas from a selected section of the Pioneer
Mountains landscape.

preexisting social and biophysical information about (for example) wildlife populations, road densities, timber harvests, and population trends.

Public feedback, social and biophysical information, and consideration of the
three aforementioned criteria enabled delineation of distinct management areas.
Integrating the various data sources meant that some management areas had boundaries that were intuitive—for example, road corridors or wilderness—while other
boundaries were less obvious, informed by people's relationships with the land and
the values and meanings associated with specific landscapes. From the 12 landscape assessments, planners devised approximately 100 management areas, each
averaging 30,000 acres (12 150 ha; see fig. 2 for an example).

Each management area carried with it a set of descriptions and prescriptions
similar to those that would ordinarily be created during the planning process. This
information was intended to be directly incorporated into the forest plan revision
and associated legal documents.

Currently (2007), the BDNF is working on its final environmental impact statement (EIS), the record of decision, and the final forest plan. Although there are aspects of the plan that draw upon the work described here, for the most part, the upfront work done with the landscape assessments has been disregarded. Place-specific recommendations and feedback were not ultimately used to develop alternatives, primarily because the planning process was not universally embraced by other stakeholders within the agency (see following section on challenges).

Benefits and Challenges of Using the BDNF is Approach

With its place-based approach, the current project sought to redefine (or add to) the scale at which forest planning typically occurs. Rather than relying on zoning standards popular in biophysical sciences (e.g., timber stands), this approach prioritized people's relationships to the land by determining the public's ideas of what constitutes "place" and defining management areas accordingly. The most challenging aspect of this project was (and continues to be) attaining buy-in from factions within the forest planning team. Much of the upfront work that was completed for this project was discounted during advanced stages of forest planning. Because place-based planning does not "fit" into any preestablished model of forest planning, disinterested parties can—if they choose—disregard recommendations altogether.

In terms of barriers within the process itself, one significant obstacle involved the EIS. The EIS gave rise to a variety of value-laden debates within stakeholder groups. Some user groups expressed concern that the identified management areas were not appropriately defined (specifically, the recommended wilderness management areas), or that recommendations for appropriate uses were problematic. Others were satisfied with these distinctions, and some intergroup controversy ensued.

In addition to debates among user groups, there was also a fair amount of intragroup conflict within landscape assessment teams. Areas of contention often centered on the concerns specialists voiced in relation to the environmental effects of human uses, particularly recreational uses. Differences in values, language, processes, and priorities led to clashes between individuals' viewpoints and inhibited progress toward final goals and products.

Originally, planners envisioned that the relationship between landscapes and management areas would be fairly seamless—bottom-up (management area to forest) and top-down (forest to management area) planning would flow naturally. The two scales were intended to be reciprocally useful in developing recommendations.

However, insights gleaned from the juxtaposition of broad- and fine-level scales were not used to inform the final forest plan. The process proved complicated and controversial, partially because the regulatory environment for developing a revised forest plan is much more stringent than the preplanning environment under which the landscape assessments and management area development occurred. However, the sociopolitical climate of the planning process—differing agendas, varied foci, and competing beliefs about how forest planning "should" occur—also contributed to the loss of much of the original detail found in the landscape and management area assessments. In the end, the final plan did not reflect scale blending to the degree that planners had originally anticipated.

In this process, the issue of scale created much contention. For many stakeholders—both public and within-agency—this project raised philosophical concerns. Although these concerns are not new to forest planners, they became more pronounced in the context of this scenario. Questions raised included: How can (or should) site-specific information and directives apply at the forest level and vice versa? Is one paradigm (forest-level planning or smaller, place-specific planning) more appropriate? Contributing to the debates about scale was the challenge of integrating different types of data. Combining discipline-specific information (e.g., wildlife data) with place-specific and forest-wide considerations presented a challenging scenario. Integrating quantitative data (e.g., projected recreation trends) with qualitative data (e.g., place meanings) added an additional layer to the mix of considerations.

Looking at the advantages of this approach, one prominent benefit was its positive public reaction. As mentioned previously, some debate arose during the EIS process. However, compared to the controversy that often accompanies planning processes, the approach was well received. Because management areas were designed to be meaningful to members of the public, citizens were able to visualize areas and, consequently, make informed recommendations about how they would prefer the areas to be managed. In this way, potential miscommunication among parties was thwarted; the relationship between planning and place became more tangible.

Along similar lines, another advantage of this approach is that it fostered dialogue among a variety of different stakeholders, stakeholders who in the past had little interaction. County commissioners, land management agencies such as the BLM, interest groups, the landscape assessment team—many of these parties worked side-by-side to reach mutual understandings of place and to determine how changes to the landscape might affect stakeholders. As a result of increased interac-

Because management areas were designed to be meaningful to members of the public, citizens were able to visualize areas and, consequently, make informed recommendations about how they would prefer the areas to be managed.

tion among stakeholders, potential conflicts were circumvented before they became problematic. Notably, the ease with which this occurred was more pronounced at the smaller, management area level; at the more abstract forest planning level, it became increasingly difficult to reach agreement and develop shared understandings.

The approach undertaken on the BDNF ultimately suited two separate (though related) goals: (1) large-scale planning—forest planning—as informed by landscape assessments, and (2) smaller scale planning—management area planning—intended to adopt a more refined vision of forest and community functioning and capture the interaction between management areas and the forest as a whole. These goals allowed for two levels of a forest plan: one targeted to individual management areas that carried with it a set of management prescriptions, the other targeted to broader, general mandates about forest operations. Having this duality of scale addressed many place-specific stakeholder concerns and permited decisions to be framed within macro- and micro-level perspectives.

For more information about the BDNF's approach, contact:

Anita DeZort
Recreation Specialist
Ashley National Forest
355 North Vernal Ave.
Vernal, UT 84078
Phone: (435) 781-5192
E-mail: adezort@fs.fed.us

Janet Bean-Dochnahl
Landscape Planner
Beaverhead-Deerlodge National Forest
Madison Ranger District
5 Forest Service Rd.
Ennis, MT 59729
Phone: (406) 682-4253
E-mail: jbeandochnahl@fs.fed.us

Chapter 3: The Willamette National Forest

Jennifer O. Farnum, Kevin Preister, and Patti Rodgers

Overview of the Area

Located in western Oregon, the Willamette National Forest (WNF) extends along 110 miles of the west side of the Cascade Mountains. Covering nearly 1.7 million acres (687 965 ha), the forest lies in proximity to several major municipalities, including Salem, Corvallis, Portland, Eugene, and Bend. Designated wilderness areas (Opal Creek, Mount Jefferson, Middle Santiam, Menagerie, Mount Washington, Three Sisters, Waldo Lake, and Diamond Peak) make up approximately one-fifth of the WNF land mass. Because of its location and climate, the WNF provides an ideal habitat for a variety of plants and animals, including threatened species such as the spotted owl (*Strix occidentalis caurina*).

Lush, mountainous terrain and the remaining old-growth forests make the WNF highly prized for its scenic value. Views of the forest's seven volcanic peaks dominate much of the landscape; its five scenic byways offer many spectacular vistas. The WNF's rivers, particularly the North and South Santiam, McKenzie, and the Willamette, are also regional icons.

Diverse recreational opportunities exist as a result of the WNF's varied geography. Some of the most popular activities include day and overnight hiking, winter motorized and nonmotorized recreation, and water-based activities such as fishing, boating, and swimming.

Project Rationale

Over the past decade, the importance of recreation in the WNF area has increased exponentially. Timber production—formerly one of the most defining aspects of lifestyles in rural areas surrounding the WNF—has decreased sharply. As a result, communities are transitioning from forest-products-based economies to recreation- and tourism-based economies. Both rural and urban areas are growing, quickly being discovered by tourists, retirees, and others looking for the types of amenities afforded by the area's natural resources.

In light of these social changes, the main goal of this project was to provide the WNF with indepth cultural and economic descriptions of communities surrounding the forest. By looking at communication networks, social and economic infrastructures, and community members' perceptions of the meanings associated with natural resources, the WNF hoped to better anticipate political trends and stakeholder needs.

Unlike some of the other case examples in this publication, the WNF project was not undertaken as a direct extension of the forest planning process. Rather, the project was initiated in order to take a proactive approach to understanding public perceptions of forest lands and surrounding communities.

Recognition of the need to better understand public attitudes arose in part owing to a pilot roads analysis conducted on the WNF several years prior to the current project. During the course of the analysis, it became evident that public opinions regarding Forest Service activities were not well understood by the agency; considerable gaps existed in terms of how accurately the agency perceived public priorities and vice versa. Thus, the WNF wanted to encourage a more personal level of public-agency interaction by providing nontraditional forums for stakeholder input.

Methods, Techniques, and Participants

This project adopted an ethnographic methodology, meaning that researchers became deeply immersed in communities in order to understand public attitudes, values, and behaviors. Researchers employed the Discovery Process^{TM}[1] to aid in their endeavors, a process premised on the idea that substantive communication occurs most effectively when members of the public are approached in everyday environments and one-to-one or small group contexts.

Before speaking with members of the public, though, researchers first had to broadly define the project's geographical scales. Based on past experience, researchers found the simultaneous use of three geographical scales to be most advantageous in conducting community studies: the **social resource unit (SRU), the human resource unit (HRU), and the community resource unit (CRU)**.

The first and largest unit—the SRU—was identified by researchers in conjunction with WNF staff and included substantial portions of western Oregon. This provided a macrolevel snapshot of the general area. The HRUs were carved out of SRUs by identifying social, economic, and geographic similarities among areas within the SRU. To make determinations regarding HRU boundaries, researchers

---

[1] This trademark is registered to James Kent Associates, a firm hired to conduct the assessment for the WNF. The Discovery Process also includes materials and tenets beyond that discussed in the current report. Contact information for the firm is provided in the final section of this case study. Note that the use of trade or firm names is for reader information only and does not imply endorsement by the U.S. Department of Agriculture of any product or service.

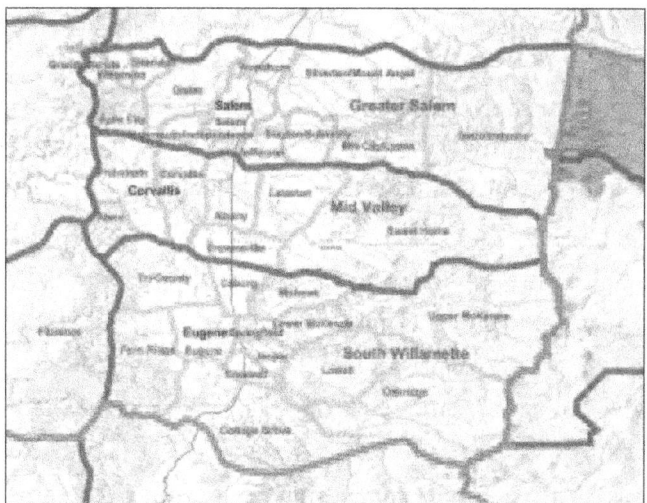

Figure 3   The Mid Valley, Greater Salem, and South Willamette
human resource units and corresponding community resource units.

assessed seven cultural indicators: publics (i.e., an identified set of people who
share similar interests or demographics), settlement patterns (i.e., the population
distribution), formal and informal communication networks (e.g., familial relationships or membership in organizations), work routines (types and location of
employment), support services (e.g., health care or law enforcement), recreational
activities, and geographic and natural features. Based on how these indicators coa-
lesced, three HRUs were formed: the greater Salem HRU, the Mid-Valley HRU,
and the South Willamette HRU (see fig. 3. Note that smaller units (CRUs) are also
delineated on this map; these units are discussed later in the chapter).

Because the area was settled east to west, settlement patterns were especially
important in forming the HRUs. Settlers "jumped" over the mountains, landing in
the Willamette Valley and then returned back to the east. Thus, the east and west
HRU boundaries are situated at the crest of mountains—the Cascade Mountains on
the east and the Coast Range on the west. These mountains divided communities
historically and are still important cultural markers in terms of differentiating
people on "either side of the hill."

Identifying SRUs and HRUs permitted researchers to enter the second phase of
the project—immersion in local communities and direct communication with the
public. Specific communities that best represented the diversity of local cultures
were selected from the HRUs for onsite information collection. Researchers then
traveled to these communities and through participant observation identified the

areas' most prominent **gathering places**. Gathering places (for example, establishments such as restaurants, gas stations, and churches) served as community hubs and presented researchers with prime opportunities to meet and interact with local residents. Because of their inclusive appeal, a variety of publics congregated at gathering places, allowing researchers to come into contact with many different types of people.

After selecting gathering places, researchers familiarized themselves with those places by getting to know owners, employees, and customers; researchers used gathering places as "base camps" for obtaining information. Engaging in semistructured, informal dialogue with community members at gathering places, researchers questioned citizens about their experiences with the area, views on public land management, priorities and challenges for the community, and other similar topics. Researchers also asked interviewees who else they should talk to—for example, previously unidentified stakeholders or those who might offer slightly different perspectives. Interviews were conducted until researchers reached a point of saturation—the point at which responses became repetitive and no new information was being garnered. Nine months were spent in this phase of the process.

> By approaching different types of people in hospitable venues, researchers were able to account for a large array of stakeholder perspectives. Based on interviews, researchers identified common themes and viewpoints shared among community members as well as domains in which community members had conflicting opinions.

By approaching different types of people in hospitable venues, researchers were able to account for a large array of stakeholder perspectives. Based on interviews, researchers identified common themes and viewpoints shared among community members as well as domains in which community members had conflicting opinions. Place meanings, place attachments, and natural resource uses and management were topics of frequent discussion. Through these discussions, researchers developed an understanding of person-specific and place-based attributes that influenced how people thought and felt about the landscape.

After considering the interview information, researchers were able to delineate CRUs based on how locals defined place. The CRUs were substantially smaller in size than HRUs and represented communities' sociocultural dynamics at a finer scale (for an example of a CRU from the Mid Valley HRU, refer to fig. 4; to view HRU and CRU scales simultaneously, see fig. 3). Larger communities (e.g., Portland, Oregon) necessarily contained more CRUs than smaller, rural communities, whereas rural area CRUs often encompassed dozens of square miles, urban CRUs were much smaller, often only consisting of a few square miles. A total of 34 CRUs were identified within the HRUs.

In the 3 months following the interviews, researchers worked on the third phase of the project: producing a major report that thoroughly detailed each of the

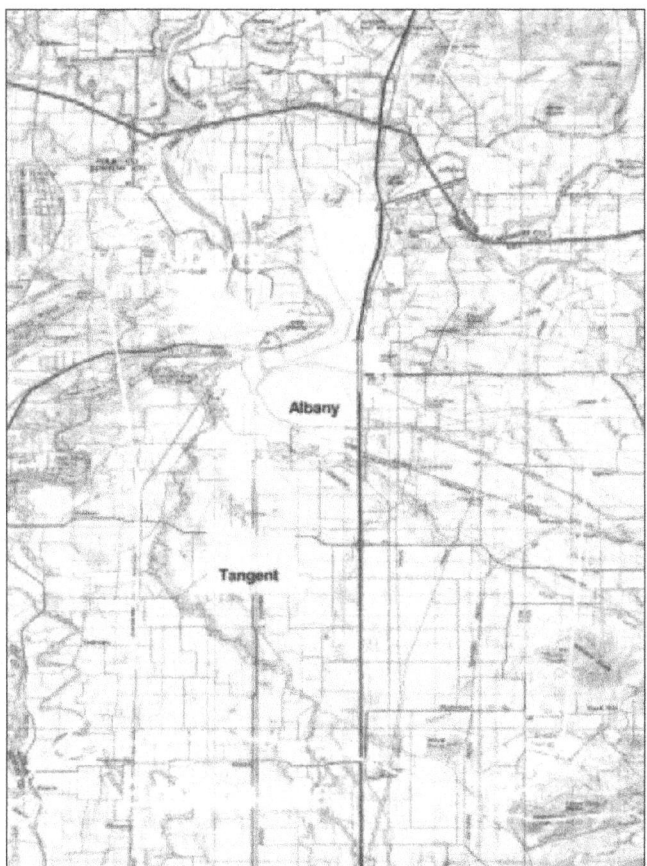

Figure 4   The Albany Tangent Community Resource Unit from the Mid Valley.

SRU's identified HRUs and CRUs via descriptors such as social and economic information, details of community life, and natural resources issues.

In addition to the report, a geographic information systems (GIS)-based tool was developed to complement research findings. The GIS software was used to overlay various forms of information such as census data, interview results, and listings of key community members. In this way, CRUs could be queried via the GIS program and different types of information viewed simultaneously.

Currently, the findings from the Discovery Process have not been formally integrated into any forest plan revisions or activities. However, the foundation for implementation remains—high quality data exist that could inform the forest plan revision. Because a considerable amount of time has elapsed since the original assessment, performing quick "check ins" with studied communities would be advisable to update existing information and reinitiate community contacts.

Benefits and Challenges of Using the WNF's Approach

One of the most substantial barriers that arose during the course of this project was the application of project findings to forest planning. As previously discussed, this project was not undertaken as an extension of the forest planning process per se but rather in hopes of taking proactive measures to understand community priorities and stakeholder assessments of public land management. However, the fact that this project was not associated with any planning directives has prevented it from being formally included in forest planning processes. Applying findings to the forest plan revision process has also been difficult owing to the transient composition of leadership teams; many of the project's original advocates have either retired or hold different positions within or outside of the agency.

Because this approach adopted an indepth, anthropological orientation to collecting and analyzing social data, there was some skepticism about whether findings exemplify "scientific" data. For many, the Discovery Process represented a paradigmatic shift in problem framing and information gathering, a shift that some viewed as unnecessary or unwarranted. Although to some skeptics the use of GIS bolstered the approach's credibility, there remained doubt as to whether the process accurately depicted public sentiment. Ironically, though, public meetings—an accepted method of gaining knowledge about public opinion—tend to breed psychological states (e.g., group polarization, groupthink) that can dilute or misrepresent individuals' true sentiments. One-on-one discussion may in fact provide less tainted portrayals of citizens' opinions.

Originally, a secondary goal of the project had been to train agency personnel in conducting social assessments (i.e., the Discovery Process). The WNF and other forests and agencies (e.g., the U.S. Department of the Interior, Bureau of Land Management) could then continue to self-assess and self-update after the original project was completed. In this way, the Forest Service and other government agencies could serve as public lands-community liaisons, enabling agencies to have clearer foresight into community priorities. Because of a variety of factors—some logistical and some philosophical—this training did not occur beyond the immediate project.

In terms of benefits of the approach, one prominent benefit is that findings were based on direct, personal, indepth contact with the public. This degree of contact provides several distinct advantages. The insight generated through personal interviews permitted researchers to form a thorough understanding of public attitudes, beliefs, and behaviors. Rather than relying on standardized, quantitative data, this qualitative approach enabled participant-driven themes to emerge through honest and direct feedback. For instance, researchers found that—contrary to common perceptions—many communities, primarily those proximate to the Interstate-5 corridor, have flourished in their transition from extraction to service-based economies. Moreover, being able to communicate personally with those involved in the transition process allowed for greater insight into community dynamics than could be gleaned through sources such as census data or newspapers.

Personal, one-on-one contact also made the emergence of social and economic trends easier to trace. Community concerns are constantly in flux and, once documented, often continue to shift and morph. Conducting face-to-face interviews provided researchers and planners with an awareness of fluctuations in attitudes and behaviors **as they were happening**; the Discovery Process allowed for in-the-moment assessment of salient public concerns as they were developing and changing.

Another advantage of this approach was its ability to use GIS to blend multiple scales and multiple social indicators. By employing this tool, geographic, social, and economic information were evaluated simultaneously, providing managers and planners with visual representations of different information types. The GIS tool also supplied managers with information about key informants for identified areas;[2] CRUs (mapped onto GIS systems) were linked to lists of community members who contributed to the assessment. In this way, agencies can track changes in attitudes and behaviors over time and develop long-term relationships with community members.

For more information about the Discovery Process/Willamette National Forest, contact:

Kevin Preister
Senior Associate
Natural Borders LLC
James Kent Associates
P.O. Box 3493
Ashland, OR 97520
Phone: (541) 488-6978
E-mail: kevpreis@jeffnet.com
Web site: www.naturalborders.com

Researchers found that—contrary to common perceptions—many communities, primarily those proximate to the Interstate-5 corridor, have flourished in their transition from extraction to service-based economies.

---

[2] Note that informants must agree to have that information made available.

Chapter 4: The Chugach National Forest

Jennifer O. Farnum and Patrick Reed

Overview of the Area

Located in south-central Alaska, the Chugach National Forest (CNF) is the second largest national forest in the United States. Over 5.4 million acres (2 185 302 ha) in size, the CNF surrounds the Gulf of Alaska's Prince William Sound. Its diverse and scenic landscapes include temperate rain forest, permanent ice and rock, highly active tidewater glaciers, and some of North America's most impressive wetlands. A number of small towns (e.g., Seward, Valdez, and Cordova) are found in and adjacent to the CNF. Anchorage, Alaska's, largest city, is located within an hour's travel north along the Seward Highway Scenic Byway.

This northernmost of national forests receives over 625,000 recreational visits annually. Visitors are attracted to such world-renowned areas as the Copper River Delta and the Kenai Peninsula. The fjords of Prince William Sound provide some of the most spectacular landscape and wildlife viewing opportunities that Alaska has to offer. During the summer months, the CNF is a prime destination for cruise ships carrying tourists from around the world.

The CNF is 98 percent roadless and accommodates an assortment of recreational opportunities such as kayaking, camping, birding, hiking, cross-country skiing, and snowmachining. Subsistence activities (e.g., gathering forest products, fishing, and hunting) are also an important draw for many forest visitors. Similarly, sport and commercial fishing are highly valued activities on the CNF.

Project Rationale

Unlike many national forests, the CNF has managed to avoid major land use disputes. Commercial timber production and mining activities have become virtually obsolete on the forest, greatly reducing the potential for land use conflicts that frequently emerge during forest planning.

Residents of surrounding communities value the forest for a wide range of reasons. Locals, including Anchorage residents, view the CNF as their "backyard" and demonstrate commendable stewardship activities geared toward maintaining the CNF's high-quality state. For example, local environmental groups frequently distribute materials praising its various qualities. Public support for the forest is so great that Alaska state governors have declared "Chugach National Forest Days" in its honor.

In the late 1990s, the CNF started its forest plan revision. As anticipated, there was considerable public support for preserving the current condition of the CNF and, by extension, retaining communities' quality of life. Accordingly, the main goal of the research project undertaken on the CNF was to investigate the type of values the public held for the forest and how proposed management alternatives might affect those values. To this end, researchers and forest planners aimed to develop a process that could systematically evaluate the compatibility of management alternatives with forest values as identified by the public. Moreover, they wanted to collect values-based data in such a fashion that the values data could be easily evaluated alongside biophysical data.

Methods, Techniques, and Participants

Working cooperatively with Alaska Pacific University, researchers administered a public values survey to a random sample of households in 12 communities adjacent to the CNF. The sampling frame was drawn from households eligible for the Alaska Permanent Fund Dividend (PFD), a program that provides Alaska residents with monies gained from investments purchased with earnings from the state's oil industry. Because the vast majority of state residents receive these funds, the PFD list provides a fairly comprehensive record of Alaska residents.[1]

The survey investigated the spectrum of values associated with the CNF. Survey items were based on 13 theory-derived, mutually exclusive value types that were listed and described on the survey: aesthetic, economic, recreation, learning, life support, biological diversity, future, subsistence, intrinsic, therapeutic, spiritual, historic, and cultural. The theory, format, and survey items were peer-reviewed by a panel of five social scientists, university faculty, and land managers from multiple agencies. The instrument was then pretested (albeit in a limited fashion) with the aid of forest staff and university graduate students.

Survey respondents were asked to apply small (1/4-inch diameter), color-coded, self-adhesive dots on a map of the CNF that was enclosed with survey materials. Dots were color-coded by value type, indicating the variety and location of their personal values for the forest.

---

[1] To qualify for PFD funds, applicants must have lived in the state for 12 months and cannot have been out of the state for more than 180 days in a calendar year.

In addition to locating value points, respondents also completed an exercise in which they indicated the relative importance of different forest values. The survey presented a hypothetical scenario in which respondents were given $100 to allocate according to their preferences for the 13 forest value types. The reported dollar figures represented the value's relative importance (e.g., assigning $25 to a specific value would indicate that the value's importance was 1/4 or 25 percent of all values reported).

More than 700 households responded (a 32 percent return rate), identifying over 15,000 value points within the CNF.[2] Values information from the returned surveys was entered into a geographical information system (GIS) database. By using GIS, researchers and forest planners obtained a general idea about how values were distributed across the forest. In this way, a visual display of spatial location of forest values (i.e., a value distribution map) was produced.

After the values distribution mapping, a **values suitability analysis** (VSA) was undertaken to examine the relationship between inventoried values and potential management actions. The VSA consisted of several steps. First, management areas were overlaid on the CNF map of value distributions. (Management areas had been identified by the forest's interdisciplinary team, or IDT, before the current research took place.) The goal of overlaying management areas with values information was to permit VSAs to be conducted separately for each management area and for the forest as a whole.

The second component of the VSA process was to compute a series of "diagnostic" statistics including a **frequency index**, a **value density index**, a **value diversity index**, and a **value identity index**. Like the values distribution mapping, **frequency** and **value density indices** were intended to provide an overview of how values were dispersed across the forest. To obtain the frequency index, the number of value points (i.e., the color-coded dots) within a specific management area was divided by the average number of points across all management areas. To determine the per-acre composition of values (i.e., the value density index) the number of value points in a specific management area was divided by the CNF's total landmass.

Value diversity and value identity indices provided finer analyses of forest values than the frequency and density indices. The value diversity index drew upon

---

[2] Although low, a 32 percent response rate is not atypical in this type of research. Also, the sample size was small but typical for surveys conducted in Alaska. Followup checks conducted for nonresponse bias suggested that participants understood the set of questions as they applied to forest plan management decisions.

the Shannon-Weaver diversity index (a tool commonly applied to wildlife and employment data) and indicated the relative composition of value types within each management area. Using advanced statistical techniques, a value identity index was calculated to assess the degree to which the distribution of values within a given management area is akin to the statistical average of all management areas considered together.

The third component of the VSA process was to evaluate proposed management activities, both individually and in combination with each other as management prescriptions. Researchers hoped to tease out whether a proposed management activity on the CNF (e.g., road construction) and management prescription (e.g., resource development) would ultimately be compatible with dominant social values (e.g., aesthetics). For this part of the process, researchers first looked at management activities and prescriptions across the CNF without regard to individual management areas. In doing so, they obtained a broad sense of activity/prescription acceptability that then could be refined by management area.

To make judgments regarding the acceptability of activities/prescriptions in relation to values, a series of matrices were constructed. Matrices required several computations. If a specific activity was deemed to be compatible with a given value, the combination received a positively weighted score (i.e., +1); conversely, if the activity was incompatible, a negatively weighted score (i.e., -1) was given. A neutral weighting (i.e., "0") was applied on occasions in which the compatibility of the activity and the value could not be easily characterized as positive or negative without more detailed information about how the activity would be carried out (see table 1).

The next step in completing matrices was to look at the cumulative value compatibility of each prescription by summing the individual activity compatibility scores. By summing the scores, each prescription received a total compatibility score (see table 2). By comparing all prescription scores, it was possible to determine the relative compatibility of each prescription with each value and to identify in rank order the best and worst matches of prescriptions and values.

Finally, a similar sequence of calculations was used to compare the compatibility of management alternatives—aggregates of management prescriptions—as applied to management areas and their inventoried distributions of values. Compatibility scores were tallied, permitting management alternatives to be ranked for each management area. In this way, various forest plan alternatives were systematically evaluated in terms of the relationships among individual management

Table 1   Weighting of compatible and incompatible activity-value relationships

Activity allowed?	Activity-value compatible?		
	Yes	**Conditional**	**No**
Yes	1	0	-1
Conditional	0	0	0
No	-1	0	1

Table 2   Relative value compatibility scores for management prescriptions

Proposed management description	Landscape value (as defined)			
	Aesthetic	**Recreation**	**Economic**	**Total**
Forest restoration	-1	0	0	-1
Dispersed recreation	1	2	1	4
Habitat improvement	-2	-1	-2	-5

activities, combinations of activities as management prescriptions, and combinations of management prescriptions as management alternatives.

An assortment of management alternatives generated by the IDT and public stakeholder groups were evaluated to see how each alternative meshed with dominant values and the distribution of all values. In sum, a total of 8 management alternatives were considered, each taking into account the relationships of the 13 value types with 42 activities in 24 management prescriptions across 94 management areas.

During a series of public meetings and IDT meetings that included members of the public, local citizens had an opportunity to validate the project's assumptions, findings, and conclusions. Question and answer sessions with the public allowed for further examination of VSA results through a type of "member' checking" in which researchers' and planners' understandings of community members' values were reviewed. In many cases, explanations of forest values and proposed management alternatives made sense to community members; in other cases, presentation of value-management information led to further debate, reevaluation of original assumptions regarding values and management alternatives, and greater clarification of the nature of value structures.

Once the VSAs were complete, alternatives had been evaluated, and public validation sought, researchers and planners were able to make specific recommendations to the IDT responsible for overseeing the CNF's forest plan revision process. However, most of the findings from the values mapping project were not included in the final forest plan revision, which was completed in 2004. The CNF constructed an interactive Web site that provides detailed information about the final forest plan revision, the final environmental impact statement, and the record of decision (see http://maps.fs.fed.us/chugach/).

Benefits and Challenges of Using the CNF's approach

The most challenging aspects of this project were two-fold: (1) developing a rational and replicable approach for collecting, analyzing, modeling, and reporting social, value-based information in a spatial context, and (2) integrating what had been traditionally viewed as qualitative, "soft" science information (i.e., values) into the forest planning process. The first challenge was the easier of the two because creating spatially explicit social values information (i.e., using GIS) was a relatively straightforward exercise that emulated traditional biophysical evaluation techniques.

The latter challenge was more problematic for several reasons. First, using the values data was perceived to be risky owing to the lack of prior experience with this type of information. How the public would receive the results was unknown and the potential legal implications daunting.

Second, promoting interdisciplinary work proved difficult. Researchers' original hope was that because social and biophysical data were presented in a similar format (i.e., GIS-based), interdisciplinary work would be encouraged— drawing upon social-biophysical information would become the operating norm for the forest planning process. However, despite the fact that the social value data was sound and emulated the format of biophysical data, there were still barriers to using the information in forest planning. Specifically, some factions within the IDT viewed the process as yielding qualitative "soft" information (bordering on anecdotal) rather than quantitative, "hard" data. The information was viewed as spurious, unsuitable for consideration in the forest plan revision. Moreover, some perceived the process as catering to public preferences while ignoring the "true" mandate of the agency—to manage biophysical resources on a sustainable basis.[3]

---

[3] Social judgments are involved in all aspects of managing biophysical resources including what sustainability entails and what it consists of; ultimately, tapping into people's value systems allows insight into sources of conflict, the types of agendas that will arise during forest planning, and how the agency can best meet the public's needs regardless of whether those needs are material, psychological, or otherwise.

The fact that there was little literature at the time that supported the methodology behind this assessment technique may have increased the reluctance of planners unfamiliar with social science to use the information in decisionmaking. Unfamiliarity may have been exacerbated by the legal ramifications of building decisions on planning processes that have not been shown to be legally defensible. Also, because there is no explicit mandate that requires forest plan revisions to fully incorporate such assessments, using values data may have appeared as an "extra" or "unnecessary" activity in an already complex and arduous process.

Although the aforementioned challenges made integrating the project's findings into the CNF's forest plan difficult, the approach taken nonetheless possesses many desirable attributes. It provides a systematic, rational method of incorporating intangible but important values into land management decisionmaking processes. Through conducting the analyses described here, social science data can be formatted to match data generated in biophysical fields. Arguably, this type of analysis requires personnel with highly specialized knowledge (e.g., statistics, GIS); ultimately, though, evaluating similar (as opposed to dissimilar) data types may help increase the comprehensiveness of the forest planning process and encourage collaborative work.

Another advantage of this approach is that it is able to quantitatively calculate the diversity of values found in a forest and in specific management areas. In determining which value types to measure, this approach borrowed from an established theory that delineates value types (specifically, Rolston and Coufal 1991; see also Brown 2005 for a more complete description of instrument development). By using this suite of values, a holistic assessment of value diversity was obtained. Planners could clearly see the spectrum of values that were associated with various places and have confidence in the knowledge that the theoretical underpinnings of the value typology are intact.

Along with the ability to capture a variety of value types comes the additional benefit of being able to identify areas that may arise as "hotspots," forest places that may be or become contentious; areas that possess a diverse set of value types may be especially important for managers to pay attention to. The value diversity index can be used to identify places that (for example) scored high on biological diversity values and also scored high on economic values—value sets that could produce opposite reactions to management decisions. This tool, then, may help explain preexisting tension or may alert planners to the possibility of future disputes. Conversely, areas with a low diversity of values and/or a small number of value points may suggest less potential for controversy.

Along with the ability to capture a variety of value types comes the additional benefit of being able to identify areas that may arise as "hotspots," forest places that may be or become contentious; areas that possess a diverse set of value types may be especially important for managers to pay attention to.

Another advantage of this approach is that it can generate management alternatives based solely on social values; the VSA can be applied both in a retrospective fashion to evaluate existing management alternatives and/or in a proactive fashion to create entirely new alternatives compatible with public values. This departs from traditional planning processes by permitting (if so desired) reversal of the normal course of planning events; in many forest planning scenarios, social implications of management actions have been acknowledged after plan revisions have been structured around biophysical considerations. The VSA permits the opposite sequencing of events, constructing plans based on social considerations that in turn may be evaluated in terms of biophysical criteria.

Lastly, this approach provides greater representativeness of public opinion than the traditional public meeting formats frequently used to meet "scoping" requirements set forth by the 1982 planning rule, which mandates public involvement in forest planning processes. Experience has repeatedly demonstrated that public meetings and other such forms of public input are subject to various forms of self-selection or nonresponse bias. Planners generally do not consider such meetings to be accurate representations of public opinion; rather, the meetings are viewed as a way to discover the nature or breadth of issues. By reaching a wider audience, the type of survey methodology employed by the CNF produces a far more representative cross section of public attitudes and beliefs than other public scoping activities that are employed.

Since the original project on the CNF was completed in the late 1990s, the value assessment approach has been adopted by several prominent organizations and institutions both in the United States and abroad. For example, the Canadian Forest Service (CFS) has applied a very similar system of value assessment to research on the social risks of wildfire. The CFS's Web-based project allowed community members to complete value assessments using online maps and materials. Similarly, the approach has been used in national park planning in Australia.

In addition to being applied in other organizations and locations, this approach has also been used in scenarios other than forest planning. These include municipal park planning, scenic highway planning, coastal management, and county-level planning. The approach's wide variety of applications across a number of different geographic places has allowed researchers and planners to assess and validate how well the approach is working. At present, both of the original project members (see contact information) are continuing to evaluate and improve the process. In doing so, they are using multiple indicators to measure technique success and are rigorously documenting progress.

For more information about the CNF's approach, contact:

Patrick Reed

Regional Social Scientist

USDA Forest Service, Region 10

3301 C Street, Suite 202

Anchorage, AK 99503

Phone: (907) 743-9571

Fax: (907) 743-9479

E-mail: preed01@fs.fed.us

Greg Brown

Associate Professor

Recreation and Outdoor Studies Department

Green Mountain College

Poultney, VT 05764

Phone: (802) 287-8330

E-mail: browng@greenmtn.edu

See also:

Brown, G. 2005. Mapping spatial attributes in survey research for natural resource management: methods and applications. Society and Natural Resources. 18(1): 17–39.

Rolston, H.I.; Coufal, J. 1991. A forest ethic and multivalue forest management. Journal of Forestry. 89: 35–40.

Chapter 5: The Grand Mesa, Uncompahgre, and Gunnison National Forests

Antony S. Cheng and Carmine Lockwood

Overview of the Area

The Grand Mesa, Uncompahgre, and Gunnison National Forests (GMUG) include approximately 3 million acres (1 214 056 ha) of federal public lands in western Colorado. Encompassing eight counties, the elevation of the GMUG ranges from a low of 5,800 feet to a high of 14,309 feet (1767 to 4361 meters). A total of 10 wilderness areas are situated within these forests, comprising approximately 19 percent of the GMUG's total acreage. Six of the Colorado 14ers, iconic mountain peaks famous for reaching heights of over 14,000 feet, are located on the forests.

A diversity of recreational opportunities are available on the GMUG. Premier trout streams and lakes are found on the forests; the Grand Mesa alone boasts over 100 lakes and reservoirs. Driving for pleasure, viewing scenery, and hiking are popular activities. Prime backcountry opportunities exist in places such as the West Elk Wilderness and the San Juan Mountains. Two world class ski resorts—Telluride and Crested Butte —attract local, national, and international visitors.

Motorized recreation, too, is popular on the GMUG, especially during the winter months when snowmobiling becomes a favorite activity. Similarly, off highway vehicle (OHV) roads and trails are found across the forests.

Project Rationale

The original GMUG forest plan was completed in 1983 and amended in 1991 and 1993. Like many other forest plans in the West, the original plan was heavily influenced by the dominant economic drivers of the era—timber production, livestock and grazing, and oil and gas exploration and development.

Today, the area's economic drivers have shifted to health care, retiree services, and recreation and tourism. This shift has arisen in part due to population growth and demographic changes in the region; United States census data show that since the early 1980s, the population of the counties within the GMUG area has increased by an average of 40 percent. Because of these changes, the GMUG wanted to approach the forest plan revision process from a fresh angle.

From the outset of the process, GMUG staff recognized that the traditional degree of public involvement in planning was insufficient and that stakeholders needed to be continually involved in forest planning throughout the entirety of the process. Staff recognized that stakeholders needed to be members of the planning process throughout its various stages and treated as coauthors in creating the forest plan revision. This recognition arose in part from work completed for the Uncompahgre National Forest's travel management plan, which took a highly collaborative approach to public involvement. As a result of that process, the GMUG became more aware of the number, level of activism, and political savvy of stakeholders.

By developing collaborative processes focused on specific places, the GMUG hoped to address a variety of critical issues. Recreation access, travel management, wilderness designation, forest health, oil and gas exploration and development, and timber management activities—all were high profile issues that were continually emerging on the forests.

Methods, Techniques, and Participants

To provide leadership during the planning process, the GMUG forest planning team worked with Colorado State University and a third-party neutral facilitator contracted through the U.S. Institute for Environmental Conflict Resolution. In addition, district rangers and their staff frequently participated in organizing and leading public meetings, a partnership that proved critical in maintaining a "connection to the ground."

Planners held a series of public workshops to gather information about how people used the land, how people conceptualized forest places, and the priorities they had for the forests. To avoid violating the Federal Advisory Committee Act (FACA), community meetings were well advertised and open to everyone. Meetings were framed as collaborative learning opportunities, soliciting a diversity of viewpoints while identifying areas of common ground.[1] As a result, many different interests were represented at meetings including those of local citizens, members of national organizations such as Trout Unlimited and the Sierra Club, and representatives from energy companies with ties to the area.

To provide a starting point for public meetings, planners divided the forests into discrete segments that the public could identify with. To this end, the planning

---

[1] A full discussion of FACA and its application to forest planning is beyond the scope of this report.

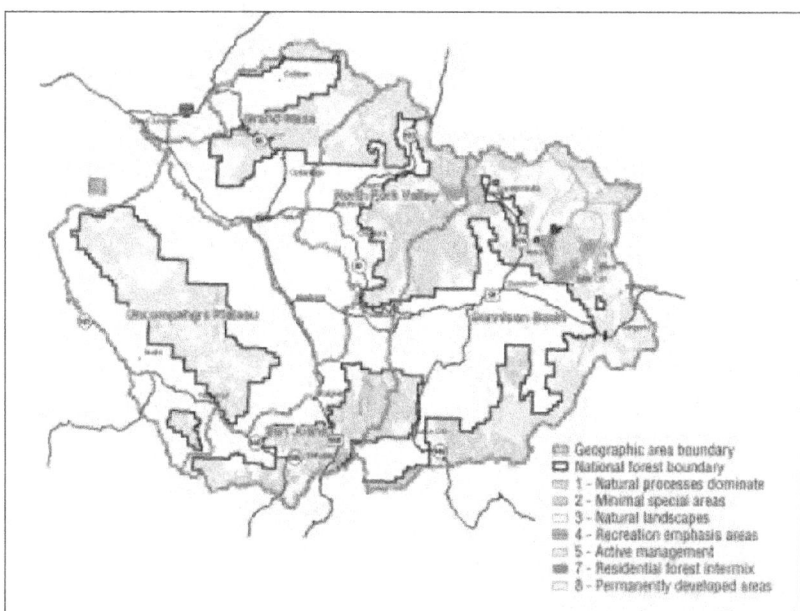

Figure 5   The Grand Mesa, Uncompahgre, and Gunnison National Forests' five geographic areas.

team worked with district staff to designate five **geographic areas** on the GMUG, areas determined primarily by topographic or watershed boundaries (fig. 5).

Once planners had developed geographic areas, the planning team and district staff held three training workshops to familiarize the public with the purpose and goals of a forest plan, principles of collaborative learning, and important forest issues. Following these introductory meetings, five Landscape Working Groups (LWGs) were convened to take an indepth look at the geographic areas; each of the geographic areas had its own LWG.

To guide the LWG procedure, leaders developed a **process monitoring strategy** in which the importance of co-constructing shared objectives was emphasized. As part of the process monitoring strategy, a series of pre- and post- meeting questionnaires were distributed to determine perceptions of the planning process and ascertain whether it was meeting participant expectations. To supplement questionnaire feedback, semistructured interviews were conducted with participants.

Adopting the tenets of adaptive management, meeting structure was continually reassessed and modified as needed, with facilitators identifying which elements to retain, which ones to adapt, and which ones to discard. To do so, GMUG staff were continuously evaluating public feedback from questionnaires and interviews, querying preexisting sources of data, and identifying areas or issues in need of further clarification.

Adopting the tenets of adaptive management, meeting structure was continually reassessed and modified as needed, with facilitators identifying which elements to retain, which ones to adapt, and which ones to discard.

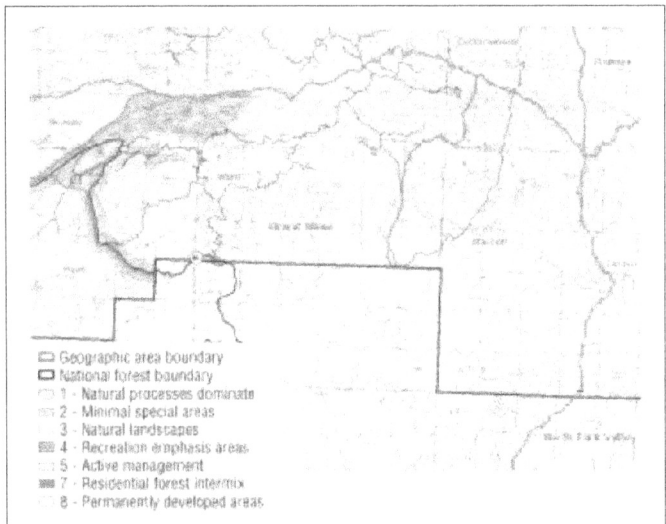

Figure 6   Examples of landscape units within the Grand Mesa and
North Fork Valley geographic areas.

Over the course of the LWG meetings, different techniques were employed to
gather and incorporate the public's perceptions of geographic areas' issues, current
conditions, and desired future conditions. For example, during the first phase of
meetings, participants determined **landscape units** and developed **vision statements**. Landscape units were small, tangible areas located within the larger geographic areas, places that groups identified as having ecological and/or social sig-
nificance. Participants often defined these units by subwatersheds, popular trail
corridors, plateaus, or distinctive landscape features that were valued by the public.
Each unit was assigned a name based on how it was known to local residents
and other users (fig. 6 shows landscape units within two of the geographic areas).
Looking holistically across a geographic area's landscape units allowed participants
to develop vision statements that articulated the geographic area's unique economic, ecological, and community niches.

To develop vision statements and encourage small group discussion, participants were divided into groups of six to eight individuals. Each individual was
asked to identify resource features and social values that make the area special—
in other words, what management guidance should reflect, emphasize, or otherwise
be attuned to. To generate this information, participants drew upon their own and
one another's knowledge of the landscape, resources, and uses, expressing their
full range of personal values for the area's social and biophysical attributes. Each
group was then asked to produce a cumulative list of the area's unique features and
values as well as opportunities and barriers for their maintenance and enhancement.

Generally, one or two meetings were required to produce vision statements that could be agreed upon by the group.

During the LWG process, the group also worked on Landscape Management Themes (LMTs), which had emerged through discussion and debate about desired conditions and suitable uses. The LMTs ranged from purely natural (i.e., conditions entirely defined by nature) to permanently developed (i.e., conditions largely defined by humans, see figs. 5 and 6). Using the LMTs, participants identified their preferences for desired future conditions and future uses for individual landscape units within the geographic area. The themes helped people to reflect upon the character of the area, what they wanted from it, and how the area is currently (and ideally) being managed.

A variety of worksheets and written materials were available to guide participants through deliberations, providing them with protocols for discussion (for examples of the various tools that were used in the visioning and LMT meetings, go to http://www.fs.fed.us/r2/gmug/policy/plan rev/collab/guides/index.shtml). Participants were encouraged to record comments and concerns, thus creating opportunities for dissenting parties to express their opinions. To aid in this process, participants were provided with:

- 3- by 5-foot maps of the geographic area divided into smaller landscape units color coded according to landscape theme dominance;
- Descriptive summaries of each landscape unit detailing its social, economic, and ecological conditions.

In all, 42 LWG meetings were conducted with 1,035 participants.

Following the final meetings, the planning team synthesized information about geographic areas and landscape units to produce preliminary versions of the proposed forest plan documents, namely the "zoning" framework of desired conditions. As advocated by the 2005 planning rule, these preliminary proposed documents were then taken back to stakeholders to complete the iterative process of plan development, review, and adjustment.[2]

Another product that emerged from the LWGs was the GMUG's **Comprehensive Evaluation Report**. This report represented the amalgamation of information regarding the forests' current conditions, trends and risks, desired future conditions, and recommended management options. Topics covered included

---

[2] Note that as this report goes to press, the United States District Court in northern California issued an enjoinment against the 2005 planning rule. How this may affect the course of the GMUG plan and other forest planning processes is uncertain.

vegetation types, number of roads and trails, recreation opportunities, potential for timber and other resource production activities, and ecological and social values. The draft version of the report was shared with the public and was further modified based on their feedback.

Although the GMUG's approach was well planned and well received by the public, the current status of the planning process outcome is uncertain. Drawing heavily upon the LWG findings, a draft revised plan was completed in summer 2006. However, it was not officially released to the public because it was withheld by the Washington office of the U.S. Department of Agriculture, Forest Service so that its compliance with the Energy Policy Act of 2005 and the 2005 planning rule could be better addressed (http://www.fs.fed.us/r2/gmug/policy/plan rev/ draft/index.shtml).

After the comments of the Washington review were incorporated, a second draft plan was released in March 2007. However, due to the ongoing legal complications associated with the 2005 planning rule, the draft plan has been suspended, and no additional public involvement work is occurring. Participants in the LWGs are anxious to learn if and how the momentum and successes of these early collaborative efforts might be recaptured once the planning proceeds under a newly approved national rule.

Benefits and Challenges of Using the GMUG's Approach

The place-based approach used on the GMUG was a highly deliberative process requiring integration of individual visions for how the GMUG should look in the future and consideration of people's roles in achieving that vision. Diverse individuals were encouraged to confront their differences, weigh relevant technical information about environmental conditions, consider the spectrum of landscape values, and develop vision statements that reflected the majority of their desires for the future management of the GMUG.

As far as barriers to the approach, four factors were most daunting. First, the LWGs were open-invitation forums. Therefore, participants and participation were somewhat variable from one meeting to the next. At times, this made continuity between meetings challenging. However, the presence of core participants—members of the public who regularly attended meetings from the beginning to the end of the process—helped to maintain consistency and bring new members up to speed on meeting history, direction, and events.

Second, the open-invitation policy employed in this approach—a policy essential to gathering diversity of views and creating a high degree of group synergy—inevitably attracted individuals who wanted to focus on a narrow agenda. Forest planning is essentially strategic planning, which precludes focusing on specific projects and issues. Some of the participants attended meetings to discuss specific projects and issues, not to concentrate on broader themes such as current and desired forest conditions. Keeping meetings centered on broader themes required ongoing vigilance.

Third, some participants lacked the knowledge necessary to focus on geographic areas and landscape units. Place-based planning relies on a certain level of spatial understanding and experience with a forest. Occasional visitors to the area would not necessarily possess this understanding but may still care deeply about its future. Thus, it was difficult to integrate the concerns of those who were invested in the GMUG but who did not have explicit knowledge of forest places.

Lastly, the budget and administrative realities facing the GMUG forest plan revision were constantly shifting. Ideally, more meetings should have been held with LWGs to complete the LMT exercises. Similarly, drafting the Comprehensive Evaluation Report took more time and effort than anticipated. Other issues such as wildfire mitigation and fuels treatment took priority over forest plan revision, diverting resources and attention away from planning efforts.

Four factors maximized the utility of this approach. The first was the upfront time devoted to preparation and planning. Cooperative arrangements among the GMUG, U.S. Institute for Environmental Conflict Resolution, and Colorado State University provided GMUG staff with additional skills and resources to design, implement, and effectively oversee the approach.

Second, the process monitoring and adaptive management strategies of the LWG process were crucial to making progress and not getting weighed down by unrealistic expectations or regulations. The resources invested in developing and implementing these strategies was worthwhile.

Third, the LWGs were able to provide substantive information to the GMUG planning team that assisted them in producing the final draft plan. Participants and planners gained a tremendous amount of knowledge about the GMUG's ecological and social landscapes. During the LWG process, participants were able to discover common ground and minimize conflicts over perceived differences. Members of the public were often surprised at how many similarities existed among themselves, other participants, and agency representatives.

Involving the ranger districts throughout the various phases of the process was vital. Having district staff at the meetings provided a degree of legitimacy and credibility in the eyes of community participants.

Lastly, involving the ranger districts throughout the various phases of the process was vital. Of the USFS staff, ranger district staff are closest to the ground and to local people who care about and use the forest. Districts often develop strong relationships with communities, so having district staff at the meetings provided a degree of legitimacy and credibility in the eyes of community participants.

For more information about the GMUG's approach, contact:

Carmine Lockwood
Forest Planning Staff Officer
Grand Mesa, Uncompahgre, & Gunnison National Forests
2250 Highway 50
Delta, CO 81416
Phone: (970) 874-6677
Fax: (970) 874-6698
E-mail: clockwood@fs.fed.us

Kathleen Bond
Neutral Facilitator
Kathleen Bond Associates
57730 Herman Road
Olathe, CO 81425
Phone: (970) 323-6577
E-mail: ktbond@aol.com

Chapter 6: Conclusion

Jennifer O. Farnum and Linda E. Kruger

We commend the researchers and forest staff who participated in developing these novel approaches to forest planning. They succeeded in finding methods of making a complicated process meaningful and relevant to the most important stakeholder in land management—the public. Across the case examples, an array of useful information was gathered, including information about the values and meanings people associated with discrete forest areas, insight into the cultural functioning of local communities, and visions for how specific areas should be managed.

Despite the ingenuity of these approaches, several practical considerations require further review and discussion. One such consideration is that place-based planning is most applicable within local contexts rather than national or even regional contexts. As noted in the GMUG case example, place-based planning requires a certain level of knowledge about an area, knowledge generally held by those who live, work, or recreate close to the area. Public lands, however, belong to the public at large; although locals may be differentially affected by forest policies, they are only one of many stakeholder groups that may be invested in the area and its policies. Indeed, during the appeal phase of a plan or project, national affinity groups often begin to assert their interests in the area, interests that may have little to do with specific places per se and more to do with (for example) the symbolic or existence value of a place. Debates such as those surrounding oil drilling in the Arctic National Wildlife Refuge highlight the fact that public land decisions can excite the interest of stakeholders on local, national, and international levels.

Another consideration raised by these examples concerns the Office of Management and Budget (OMB). Researchers employed by the federal government are well aware that many mechanisms of communication with the public require "OMB clearance" or, in other words, adherence to the Paperwork Reduction Act (PRA) of 1995. The PRA is intended to both minimize the burden placed on the public during government data collection processes and ensure the quality and integrity of collected information. Although the PRA was not intended to apply specifically to the 1982 planning rule (which requires public input in forest planning processes), there is ambiguity regarding the extent to which the PRA may pertain to some techniques used in place-based planning. Specifically, PRA regulations clearly stipulate that any survey, interview, or focus group scenario involving 10 or more members of the public must undergo OMB evaluation and authorization (see http://www.archives.gov/federal-register/laws/paperwork-reduction/). A full discussion of how and to what degree OMB considerations may apply in place-based planning approaches (or forest planning generally) is outside the scope of this report; however, such considerations should be fully evaluated when planning for the cost, time, and legal ramifications of employing these and similar approaches.

An additional hurdle in conducting place-based planning is that such approaches tend to generate a considerable amount of information—even more information than traditional planning processes, which are already lengthy and complex undertakings. Consider the example of the Willamette National Forest: The final report given to the forest was well organized and well summarized—and based on a large amount of qualitative data. Without management personnel who are highly invested in the process and who have access to staff and funding to support the effort, the amount of accessible information may have been perceived as unmanageable. In the case of the Chugach National Forest, too, the agency's willingness to implement findings may have been tempered by a high volume of "nonessential" information. Because social systems are complex and require high levels of monitoring and iterative reassessment, investing in place-based planning processes may seem like an unnecessary use of resources.

Looking at the marginal "success rate" of the four examples, is the amount of time, effort, and resource expenditure justified? Put another way, is the value-added through these types of processes worth the cost? At this point in the development of place-based planning, those answers are unclear. Research on place-based planning has (like many grassroots efforts) tended to be spurious, often times lacking the type of scientific rigor that it will take to make valid, substantive decisions about the strengths and weaknesses of the variety of place-based approaches. Approaches need more indepth research, research that uses critical, evaluative methods and employs strict methodological standards. Blending quantitative and qualitative data collection techniques should also be used to advance a more complete perspective of social and biophysical conditions while cross-validating data types.

From a planning perspective, concentrating on producing such robust research may seem superfluous—even daunting—which is why developing planning-research relationships (e.g., among forests, research stations, and universities) can be beneficial. Planners gain a better quality product, while researchers are able to build upon specific examples, cross-pollinating findings and further enhancing the general fashion in which place-based planning can and should be carried out.

> **Approaches need more indepth research, research that uses critical, evaluative methods and employs strict methodological standards. To advance a more complete perspective of social and biophysical conditions while cross-validating data types.**

Determining whether place-based planning is a beneficial endeavor for forests requires evaluation of the social, political, and financial environments within which each forest is operating. Units that do opt to implement place-based planning in some form or fashion will benefit from the following suggestions:

1. Develop relationships with researchers. Scientists at research stations, universities, and private firms may be interested in working with planners to refine the process and document results.

2. Before planning processes are implemented, seek the advice of planning team members and those in higher levels of management who will incorporate the results into legal documents and sign off on the final plan. Regardless of the approach's merit, there will almost always be some form of dissent; as those in the field of marketing point out, ideas do not "sell themselves."

3. Present suggestions for place-based approaches in their formative rather than finalized stages. Not only does this allow for the inclusion of fresh material from the project's inception, but it also ensures that members of the planning community feel that they were appropriately consulted and their views were adequately considered. In turn, this raises member vestedness in the process.

4. Gain support and feedback from members of the larger place-based planning community. Many involved in the Portland workshop expressed feelings of isolation, of being unaware of others who were conducting similar work. Networking with like-minded individuals (e.g., through the information listed in this publication) can be psychologically reassuring and also provide direction for planning from start to finish.

In the approaches described in this publication, place-based planning was used as a mechanism for understanding public values, meanings, and place attachments. Often times, this resulted in the prioritization of recreation activities, aesthetic integrity, or existence values. However, there is no inherent aspect of place-based planning that requires this to be so. Rather, the most useful aspect of place-based planning may be that it insists that planning occur at scales that have meaning to the public rather than (for instance) scales based on timber stands. Within these socially meaningful scales, discussion of priorities can be better framed, regardless of whether the results of such discussion ultimately champion recreation, extraction, or other activities or uses. Naturally, there may be occasions when place "boundaries" that are meaningful to the public will need to be expanded or contracted, particularly when thinking about wildlife corridors, regional planning, threatened and endangered species, and other intangible services that are afforded by public lands. Nevertheless, place-based planning can serve as a tool in reconceptualizing the way that planning units are developed; overlaying values and "place interest" information side-by-side with other types of data can provide more nuanced information about management opportunities and challenges.

Despite their potential usefulness in some arenas of public lands planning, place-based approaches are far from a cure-all for difficulties encountered in planning processes. Rather, the value-imbibed, meaning-rich information gleaned from place-based approaches should be treated as one (albeit important) consideration in planning. Other considerations—wildlife habitat, timber production, water quality, airsheds, threatened and endangered species, etc.—must continue to be appropriately weighted in successful planning endeavors.

Place-based, collaborative approaches represent necessary and timely alternatives to traditional forest planning processes. With the emergence of value-centered planning and increasing environmental awareness within the American public, there seems little possibility that extraction- and production-related priorities will dominate forest planning processes to the degree they once did. Compared to early grassroots efforts to make adjustments to forest planning procedures, place-based approaches have made great strides in terms of both their methodologies and scale. Employing place-based approaches allows for dialogue to occur at socially meaningful scales, thereby incorporating landscape values and embedded landscape meanings and taking a necessary step in developing holistic planning approaches that are truly adaptive.

Acknowledgments

This research is part of the Recreation and Tourism Initiative. Funding came through the Focused Science Delivery Program and The Human and Natural Resource Interaction Program of the Pacific Northwest Research Station.

The editors would like to thank Antony Cheng for his help in designing and facilitating the workshop and the workshop participants for sharing their experiences. We also appreciate the effort and aid of the co-authors and the reviewers who contributed to this publication, Gerard Kyle, Jamia Hansen-Murray, Chris Hansen-Murray, and Dale Blahna. They were especially helpful in the development of the "Conclusion" section.

www.ingramcontent.com/pod-product-compliance
Lightning Source LLC
Chambersburg PA
CBHW080616290526

45790CB00007B/2797